Inside Outrage

Poems

Gary Glauber

Copyright © 2022 Gary Glauber

Author photo, Copyright © 2022: Zane Glauber
Cover art: © 2022 Loree Harrell, *Digging A Hole In Tomorrowland*

ISBN: 978-1-7354002-9-7
Library of Congress Control Number: 2022930020

Published by Sheila-Na-Gig Editions
Russell, KY
Hayley Mitchell Haugen, Editor
www.sheilanagigblog.com

ALL RIGHTS RESERVED
Printed in the United States of America

Acknowledgments

Many thanks to the kind editors of the following journals in which these poems first appeared:

Amethyst Review: "The Nature of Inquiry"
Ariel Chart: "Dance in Four Movements," "Deep in the Canyon," "Polaroid," "Practicum"
BlogNostics: "Call of the Damaged"
Blue Heron Review: "Long Shot"
Bowery Gothic: "Requiem: Before You"
Caliban Online: "Classic Takedown"
Cirrus Poetry Review: "And There Was Light"
Cultural Weekly: "Luggage," "The Unearthing"
Event Horizon Magazine: "Perpetuity"
Every Pigeon: "Resolution"
Foliate Oak Literary Journal: "Excellence is our Motto"
HCE Review: "Welcome to Amorica"
Indiana Voice Journal: "Baggage Claim"
Koan – Paragon Press: "Steinweg's Erosion"
Kool Kids Press: "Talking"
KYSO Flash: "Three Feet and a Yard"
MacQueen's Quinterly: "Storming the Beaches in Organdy"
Mojave River Press + Review: "Holiday Apothegms," "Meeting Joan of Arc for Brunch," "Dancing for Lions"
Muddy River Poetry Review: "Expedition"
New Verse News: "Intolerance Afternoon," "Hey Nineteen," "The Classroom"
Pamplemousse: "Sad Burlesque," "Peripeteia"
Panoply: "Special Carousel"
Sheila-Na-Gig online: "Errand Boy," "Bird in Springtime," "Bildungsromantic," "Medusa," "Aquarium," "Morning Confession," "Senescence," "History's Assurance"
Stoneboat Journal: "The Progression"
The Courtship of Winds: "Inveigled"
The Flatbush Review: "Consecration"
The McKinley Review: "Homestead"
The Piker Press: "Downhill Racing," "Game With No Shot Clock," "Napoleonic Code"
The Scene & Heard Journal: "Habits of Love and Consequence"

The Song Is…: "Artifice"
The Writers' Café: "Logography"
Tuck Magazine: "Recipe for Disaster"
Verse-Virtual: "Dear Invisible Oppressors," "Albert's Lament," "Big Reveal," "Blocked"
Watershed Review: "The Favorite Fish is the Dead Fish"
Writers Resist: "Planet of the (r)Apes"
Your Daily Poem: "Interior Motive," "Work Desk Sacrament"

The business of the poet…is to show the sorriness underlying the grandest things and the grandeur underlying the sorriest things.

~ Thomas Hardy

Contents

I. IN

Welcome to Amorica	12
Inveigled	13
Errand Boy	15
Dance in Four Movements	17
Homestead	19
Luggage	20
Sad Burlesque	21
Call of the Damaged	23
Bird in Springtime	24
And There Was Light	25
Dear Invisible Oppressors	26
The Progression	27
Artifice	28
Deep in the Canyon	30
Napoleonic Code	31
Intolerance Afternoon	32
Logography	34
Hey Nineteen	35
Classic Takedown	36
Polaroid	37

II. INSIDE

Special Carousel	39
Interior Motive	40
TripTik	42
Habits of Love and Consequence	44
Consecration	45
Baggage Claim	47
Albert's Lament	49
Recipe for Disaster	50
Bildungsromantic	52
Medusa	54
Big Reveal	55
Resolution	57
Storming the Beaches in Organdy	59
Aquarium	61
Change of Seasons	62
Game With No Shot Clock	63

III. INSIDE OUT

Long shot	65
Planet of the (r)Apes	67
Learning to Read	70
Downhill Racing	73
Requiem: Before you	74
The Favorite Fish is the Dead Fish	76
The Human Filigree	78
Dancing for Lions	79
Holiday Apothegms	80
Steinweg's Erosion	82
The Work Desk Sacrament	83
Elegy for Lost Alliance	84
Morning Confession	86
Excellence is Our Motto	87
The Nature of Inquiry	88
Senescence	89

IV. INSIDE OUTRAGE

Peripeteia	91
The Unearthing	93
Practicum	96
Three Feet and a Yard	97
Talking	98
Perpetuity	100
Blocked	102
Legerdemain	103
The Classroom	104
Meeting Joan of Arc For Brunch	106
Expedition	108
Have You Graded The Essays Yet?	110
History's Assurance	111
Inside Outrage	112
Re-Cycled	113
Notes	116
About the Author	117

Dedicated to the memories of Peter Heinegg, who elevated smart into art, and Jason Sheroan, my brother in power pop.

&

For all the remaining readers and believers

I. IN

Welcome to Amorica

Love's language spoken here,
the in-shop window sign proclaims,
as if such proclamation were equivalent
to *open* or *closed*: informational, helpful.

He whispers into electronic translator
but no kiss forms from sounds passing
in stark stale air of dipthongs and digraphs
lingering with longing, then gone.

I'm here for the conversation, he declares,
as the door chimes shut behind him.
*I want to pluck deep-seated emotions
from their arcane inner hiding places.*

Conversion occurs in a sated nation.
Quickened breath and fevered pitch
are thrown for loss in a pluperfect world
with infinitives stretched to infinity.

You really know how to talk, she notes.
He voices a phoneme phenomenon
and she murmurs her sweet approval.

Sentences are spoken,
fricatives flowing fast in lavender air,
as if remembering that very first word
and the bond bounding beyond it.

The hour is reflected
in two hungry mouths,
wide open, tongues awaggle,
weak with speaking.

Inveigled

He gingerly takes first step,
careful not to stumble,
not knowing beyond that door
lay a universe of curious troubles.
Silk batiks hung over windows,
beads replacing doors and
the color red dominant —
bleeding through as if
claiming territory, crowding out an
unwanted spectrum of colors,
a flag of caution, of warning,
but he felt the opposite,
drawn to this eclectic warmth,
this claustrophobic tableau,
bearing olfactory witness
to a unique mix of musk
and powder and incense.
The walls hung with
unfamiliar paintings,
dark scenes from distant mountain hovels
with odd clusters of nameless hordes.
They gathered in shadows
to negotiate hard lives
of labor, grit, and compromise.
Even their horses looked grim.
This ramshackle studio,
bastion of small mirrors
and tables holding framed photos
of unsmiling people in
other century's clothes,
a clipped pile of receipts
by a burgundy checkbook.
And barely visible,
in the next small room over,
her bed, beautifully appointed,
an inviting exhibition of

soft pillows and knitted throws,
a prize taunting and teasing,
an intimate diary page revealed,
a destination of desire.
He came to that space
hoping to know her intimately,
to convince with charm and panache,
a hunter in search of prey.
Now, disarmed, he whirls in
strange recesses, thrown akimbo
by this derelict den of exotic enigma,
transformed, transfixed,
seducer now seduced.

Errand Boy

I carry out the trash
and with it an unburdening
of suburban responsibilities,
careful care of tended lawn,
weight of native souls long gone
from formerly forested high ground.

I am haunted with
afflictions of love, desires
to simplify mortgage
and insurance shackles,
shady cloud formations
slow dancing across
fading cerulean sky.

This is the pedal steel's
low wail of sweet longing,
open tuning that invites
unassuming ear to listen.
This is how weeds invade
gardens, how those sporting antlers
make scant winter meals last,
how lush growth morphs into
bright blinding bleak terrain.

I sing along with coyote pack's yowls,
gooseflesh raised in reflexive salute,
bloodlust of the wild unleashed
toward unsuspecting moon.
Martyrs of the makeshift unite,
sliding over black ice toward
dark inevitable, eyes closed
to hymn of engine thrum,
careening anthem-like chorus
calling Aeolus from afar.

Rust never oxidizes here
and everything stays just so,
Currier & Ives with an
insider's nod and wink.
The cans stand at end of driveway,
innocuous bystanders like
ancient seers, lifted and emptied,
but back again brimful with insights,
same time the very next week.

Dance in Four Movements

I.

When they first dance,
he has no real knowledge of dancing.
The steps are hesitant, clumsy, remote,
showing a beginner's awkwardness.
Inside, his heart dances
with great elan and flair,
a flame flickering with ignorance.
There is a great bounty yet of hope.

II.

They meet again in a foreign land
and the grand dance resumes.
She pretends not to have followed him there.
Their bodies now understand the interplay,
energy and inertia, the mingling and grace.
It is a dance of greed and desperation,
of long history and swaying need.
Their eyes meet and they carefully proceed.
She follows his lead, the movements
bring happiness, even if it is only illusion.
Such perfection is never real.
They thank the terpsichorean muse
before parting this pas de deux.

III.

Years later, he is dancing alone.
He thinks back with gratitude
on his partner from kinder years.
He is devoted to the memories,
the steps and routines, how this
discipline freed him from the usual,
the love that might tumble to grief.

IV.

The old man can only manage
a few brittle moves. The turns
are now accompanied by pain.
He gives his best to venture a dance
for all the dreams long faded.
Spinning jumps sputter forth,
mere shadows swapped for passion.
He knows the steps, but body
refuses, and he learns anew
sorrow of limits' bewilderment.
He yearns for that first dance,
and a lifetime of learning,
one imperfect step at a time.

Homestead

Within dusky shadows,
besieged by his voice
still inside your head,
you try to hide.

Books with lessons
cascade like waterfalls,
those scarred hands
still punctuating stories

as if restless gestures
could compel listeners
to rapt attention,
motion as magnet.

His reassuring baritone
silenced now forever,
that aural kiss of certitude
clear as corner office glass.

Residue of memory lingers:
that favorite chair's leather
touched with impression
as if he only just got up.

Still holding tiny hand
inside insulated mittens,
guiding you across intersection
like sun in afternoon sky.

Remembering exhausts you:
days, weeks, years
accrued with no interest,
now suddenly gone into

empty bottle's endless night
of silent refrain. You crack a window,
stare into darkness, wait for eternity
to surrender a clue.

Luggage

I unpack the suitcase of your absence with care,
an act of dissolution, ablation, penance, rotation.
Once this world teemed with a million you,
now the sun's bleak stare raises an eyebrow,
questioning my every move, clambering along
hallways and byways trying to escape memories:
ceilings we ignored, mirrors that opened
to our happiness, the fleeting contentment of
our conjoining, distant sounds of lilting laughter.
I awake to new universe, cold and forgotten,
unfamiliar, unknown. Points of light dance
in deep shadow, mocking movements of
former grace, now stilted and forced,
a song without lyrics, a cloud of empty aims.
One compartment for excuses, another for alibis.
Yet there's no stopping those who shall judge,
offer up false knowledge, opined and orated,
charlatan tonics that cure nothing at all.
The ice melts my anger, and I am left
sipping thoughts like marrow, wishing for
before, trading reflections for affection,
sorting through the lack and lachrymose,
item by item, putting it all away.

Sad Burlesque
For EC

It's not for everyone.
The eclectic nuanced wail,
the lyrical bravado of
innuendo, double entendre,
badinage and bonhomie.
An assault on several senses
that caught enough popular sway
once upon an earlier time
of bitterness and angry young men
fighting to find their place.
Now, forty years and
a shelf full of releases after,
some are willing to read
this lengthy firsthand account.

This musical chameleon,
student of sundry genres and styles
has ventured bravely forth
in a wide swath of directions
with mixed results, but always
with most sincere intent
to capture and illuminate
the unsung genius of others.
That man with many heroes
and an unyielding love for his father
was once hero to me, a beacon
whose music could guide me
through often rocky shoals
of tempestuous adolescence.

But this wavering aural dynamite,
champion of emotional strife,
has long since lost righteous rage.
Years of unhappy, inexplicable choices
are glossed over in this retelling,

supplanted with chapters focused
on celebrity collaboration,
poignant celebrations for noble causes,
galas punctuated with lyrical snippets.
The once fierce and feral genius
has been tamed, full ferocity removed
and replaced with this domesticated
and reflective father of three,
sanded down by winds of experience,
become more quietly wise and wry;
such is the transformative power of life.

Call of the Damaged

A curtain of darkness surrounds her,
beyond Goth fashion sensibility
and the striking beauty she has grown into,
heightened by hesitancy and pain.
The past attack has scarred her for life.
That night some tornado of ignorance
subsumed and corrupted her, innocence
turned into thick net of constant resistance.
She has become the void within torn holes,
retaining the shadow ugliness, pushing away,
limbs akimbo, against encroaching storm
always encroaching. See, weather is a constant:
there are fronts of men to confront,
be affronted by. Daily ache of memories
fuels lightning behind trenchant eyes,
windows to injured soul,
where past rain puddles and pools,
a world of hurt these hard shots
cannot easily erase.

Bird in Springtime

It's always you at the door
sprouting some new declaration,
blue with brash enthusiasm,
loved and over-encouraged.
My place becomes a shrine
to you via careless remainders,
books, videos, post-its
to remind (that you since forgot).
You are the constant
matched up with fresh x factors,
wild cards that repel as vortex,
sending you back always different:
drunker, wiser, older,
more likely to lose your way.
Yet internal compass returns you
like swallows to Capistrano,
licking wounds and riding winds,
wanderer turned mighty worrier.
Again, batty battle ensues,
and when you knock, I answer,
recipient of your comings, then goings,
welcome mat for well-traveled narrative,
knave to your fickle vixen's visits,
forgiver of seasonal sins.

And There Was Light

Silence is always an argument for the opposition.
I had to speak up to stand a chance, to save
what was left of my past glory and grandeur.
This was no celebration. There would be no
fireworks following. No fife. No drums.
The long stairs leading to the church was
where Katie and her friends would smoke
and pretend to be too cool for school.
I went mute on the matter. It was all too strange.
Wave the flag and hope the odd denizens salute.
They are more concerned with their own problems.
"Beauty is no longer a thing," she told me,
and her court robes made me believe it.
There were crowds in the upstairs gallery,
looking on, snickering at my confusion.
I wanted to read them my resume, show them
what an ordinary man might manage to accomplish.
"How do you plead?" asked the colossal security officer.
It was accidental, the same way one might look away
for a minute and miss the end of the world.
Like so many recent dreams, this one defied logic.
I wasn't sure what I was being charged with,
only that I already owned the accompanying guilt.
I cleared my throat, cleared my mind,
and started vocalizing any Bible stories
I could remember, hoping they might
provide necessary solace, but all the
names kept coming out wrong, all wrong.

Dear Invisible Oppressors

First off, thanks for keeping things so competitive.
We blame it on karma, on mercury's retrograde,
on bad luck and errant wrong beliefs, but I know
you're hard at work, doing your unsung tasks,
preventing and debilitating honest efforts
like clockwork, getting regular results in a
highly professional manner. What do you get
in return? Lambasting invective and anger.
Don't they realize that sometimes
prevention *is* the cure? Disappointment
is a lifestyle choice, thanks to you.
It's been a privilege to see your subtle
insinuation, your negative nuance,
your way of putting reward at a safe and
unapproachable distance. Genius.
Not all downtrodden get defeated.
We who persist must be challenged anew,
time and again. It's not just a simple
accumulation of 10,000 hours,
as Malcolm suggests. Not when such
unseen forces are working Newton's
equal and opposite. Know that there's
at least one admirer, appreciating
how you keep achievement at bay.
Kudos to you; keeping up the forever
quicksand struggle. It's been something
being stuck like this, moving in circles
that always bring us back to square one.

The Progression

Nothing is lost yet. A scintilla of hope rides the north wind.
And admit it, you love how those branches comingle.
Forest speaks to you in breath of bird chatter and memories.
In a way, it recreates you. Puts you where you need to be.
You admire this trunk's heft, the statement of power it exudes.
This is the center of now, here of where, mystery of the known.
Nature is a persuasive stranger, one you hope to soon befriend.
Skunk cabbage heralds new spring, a chance to be better.
Ravens seem to mock your circuitous path through these woods.
You ignore them and plod forward, finding your footing
by reassurance of heading somewhere, guided by sky and sound.
These trees are brethren, looking out for your welfare,
silent spectators to this process, this halting motion,
moving headlong on this journey, twelve steps at a time,
walking until found.

Artifice

The smoked glass
is polarized,
guaranteed to protect
in ways the naked
eye could never.
Soon the show begins,
moon incrementally
overtaking shining red sun
for the momentary victory.
But before darkness
worries the local birds
into frightful screeching,
I pretend to read an article
that might enlighten me
about the private life
of a renowned filmmaker
whose dark bizarre works
inspire me. He is strange
and controlling and ruinous
in his choices, something
of a bellicose tyrant
and unpredictable.
This is not surprising.
You have to boil water
to make rice, he says.
He is quite demanding,
even in his domestic tasks.
Thinking back to some
of the more harrowing scenes,
the unspoken terror
mastered through
camera's eye
is mesmerizing.
Iron-clad principles
run rampant
through rusty lives

of weaker types.
Such people cannot
hide, overtaken by
the wild's vim and vigor,
unmasked with each
raspy breath, exposed
in their hiding spots,
disturbed and about
to be forever changed.
Darkness prevents
me from reading more,
yet the sun will be back
and the world will continue,
red blood pumping hard
through four chambers
much as it has before,
world revealed as
no different than
a good hearty
bowl of rice
served well,
life as simple
as the salvation
of using chopsticks
properly.

Deep in the Canyon

There are only so many fingers
you can hold up to remind me.
Life was one big emergency then.
Harsh fluorescent lights
seeped through sadness,
illuminating deserted items
that littered the landscape
of two hearts gone awry
and further, why.
We had mistaken time
for opportunity, a frenetic
chase from absence to alibi,
a convenient arrangement
that benefited none,
and was suddenly done.
Three thousand miles,
the plaintive cry of
jilted lovers, stipulations
of bitterness as vanity,
and you claim insanity.
The rollercoaster climbs slowly,
but oh that drop soon arrives,
takes your breath away.
Begging for leniency,
pleas and thank you, indecency.
A faded photo you
show nosy neighbors
when and if they show.
It's a lonely life now
exploring the hollows
and all that soon follows.

Napoleonic Code

This no-win decision
tests blood's allegiance.

After devastation and betrayal,
how does one behave?

Passion spills into perversity,
an ape show of vigorous pride.

This is what comes from
silk shirts and poor life choices,

territory and columns
marked for certain destruction.

Respectability battles urges;
a shot glass serves as home.

Extinguish the light,
prevent the lurid reflections.

She came a long way to interfere,
hiding from her own flaws.

Two of a kind spiraling
into a realm beyond reason.

Music triggers memories,
a shot rings out; a bottle breaks.

Shaking stars from the sky
doesn't much calm the nerves.

Fate delivers abuse
and what could have been
is what shall never be.

Intolerance Afternoon

No one wanted to wait on the mermaid.

I couldn't believe the rudeness.
She was out of her element,
waiting on this long line
nowhere near the water.
The barista acted like
she wasn't even there.

But she was. Patiently waiting
her turn, eager to order.
She deserved her vanilla latte
as much as the next guy,
who happened to be me.

I had been behind her,
trying to pretend I didn't
notice her resemblance
to the national chain's logo:
same enchanting smile,
same long locks of hair.

Did they not hear
that uniquely dulcet tone,
the unmistakable foreign accent?

I stood there mute
when they passed her by
and turned to me instead.
I refused to be party
to this obvious act
of blatant prejudice.
What was the deal?
No shirt, no legs, no service?
No way.

Her scales glistened in
what I perceived was anger
or at least righteous rage.
It reminded me of that time
at the barbershop
when they refused service
to the giant who stopped in
for a trim.
They said it was
by appointment only,
and ignored the way
he barely fit into the chair.
He sat there for a time,
all awkward knees and elbows,
but these barbers were a stubborn lot.
He looked at me, shrugged his shoulders,
let out an exasperated sigh, then got up.
Something in the look
told me he got this a lot.
There's small,
and then there's petty,
was what he said
before storming out.

When I finally opened my mouth
it was with fast solution at hand.
I spoke out the very order
she had been repeating
over and over again,
followed by my own.
I spoke slowly and the barista
repeated it back.
I gladly paid for hers,
and was happy to hand over
the green and white cup
a few minutes later,
not so much as an act
of flirtatious friendliness,
but more one of
true civil justice.

Logography

It was a time of infinite complication,
all points on the spectrum possible,
an epidemic of false information
featuring science as sentiment,
facts commensurate to fiction.
All that had gone before was going,
fading fast in a blizzard
of ethical impropriety,
millionaires posing as gatekeepers
putting self-interest ahead
of the myth of greater good.
Narcissus laughs atop Mount Helicon
as we descend into a valley of
stunned disbelief, each succeeding
day's developments challenging
status quo into quo vadis,
a seismic disturbance
that threatens to topple
tenets and safe foundations.
Righteous outrage points fingers
at what's being brushed
under collective carpet
and still, no one hears
or especially cares.
At least the sun rises,
but that whisper on the wind
is likely old Herodotus,
turning fitfully in his grave.

Hey Nineteen

It's all fun and games until someone loses an eye.

A student is proud of his clever renaming of the virus.
He calls it "The Boomer Remover."

It's all fun and games until the coughing goes dry.

One with the sniffles sneezes
and the kids around him yell "Corona!"

It's all fun and games until the fever runs high.

One kid has been to a conference where several have since
been identified as having the virus. "Why are you here?" I ask.
"Don't want to forever be known as that patient zero kid
who infected everyone else." "But you are," I think.

It's all fun and games until there are no more cleaning supplies.

Another kid claims his uncle has it because he saw the doctor
that first saw the lawyer before he was sent to the hospital.
There are at least ten similar stories I hear
throughout the course of the school day.

It's all fun and games until everything's canceled on the fly.

If most kids can easily survive it, they start out oblivious
to what they might be bringing home to grandparents or parents.
Still, a few days later, some register concern,
while others start to panic.

It's all fun and games until so many people die.

Classic Takedown

A leg kick seems apropos
in light of tangled negotiation;
the sucker punch of realization
dawns upon those in-the-know.
We call it hobby knowledge,
this advice pieced together
from strands of flowering sedge
and wind-dispersed feather.
Open wide and gather seeds
that dictate what should follow.
There's profit in ignoring needs
by light of fading tallow.
Waiting, talking on the fly
about what breaks will signify.
Crises we cannot ignore:
broken and asking for more.

Polaroid

In the end, small details
reveal the hidden story.
The pointless journey undertaken,
the heartbreak of refused entrance,
the litany of woes and troubles
that pursued her for years after.
In the photo, she smiles,
acknowledging unspoken volumes.
The nuance of weakness
like ticking time bomb,
testing the very concept of courage.
All this, all for one,
all for the cause of fanaticism
dressed up as innocence.
You swallow hard, try to recall
where it was taken, circumstances
that memory won't reveal:
fuzzy at best, a brief toehold on
the cascading collapse
that was already well on its way.
The waterfall of disappointment,
a love painful in its simplicity,
concealing great despair
behind powders and creams.
This was an instant in time,
blanket placed carefully
as something to hide behind,
a gesture to modesty,
pitiful keepsake transformed
into sentimental memento.
She is gone forever,
and you struggle to hold
these possibly poignant memories
from the inevitable, indomitable
slow fade to black.

II. INSIDE

Special Carousel

He didn't like the hard horses
and the benches left him
nonplussed.
Given a choice
he preferred the secret box,
the singular tiny one-seat room
of total darkness.
He would enter quietly
and close the door behind him,
safely ensconced,
protected from calliope
and flashing lights,
a peaceful place
within artificial stampede.
As others call out
pretend cavalry
in search of golden ring,
he feels motion in safer silence,
acknowledging the reality
of going nowhere
in the black void of a dream
like the inside of an eyelid,
feeling only heartbeat's thrum
as poled horses dance away
in some distant frantic universe
just outside his reach.

Interior Motive

Intellect doomed me
to be an indoor person,
pacing in front of classrooms,
encouraging thought beyond
what appears on the page.
This is my stage, my loading dock,
my spot on the academic assembly line,
the place where I share my passions
whenever curriculum allows.
It is the meeting place for
disparate generations,
old school and new,
taking shots across the bows,
then texting back replies.
Waning attention spans
focus on grade point averages
that someone somewhere
convinced them can be negotiated.
I dissuade them of that notion,
instead encouraging improvement
of skills by which to earn
credits enough to avoid
that slippery slope
of complaint and confusion.
This is the age of enabled winners,
coddled and boosted up
to dizzying heights, and I am
the town crier, announcing
the harsh reality in red pen
late at night over essays
that invite analysis
beyond formulaic response.
This is no world for the weak,
but effort goes a long way
toward sharpening
that serpent's tooth

into an eventual appreciation
of why literature matters
and a someday gratitude
for all this indoor effort.

TripTik

He always seemed reclusive, remote,
as if removed at a great distance.
Like Pavlov's dog, I hear a bell ring
and I think of him, of the sky, the rooftops
turning black inside summer's late dusk.
Inside, it's hot, hotter than usual
in this mid-year's reflexive reflection.
That bright red dress with small flowers
translating to movement, the motion of grace.
This is Ana Song, he said. *My friend*.
She always spoke of towers on high hills,
places she might visit someday.
Thinking of the future moves anything along,
but details of the past slow our progress.
Twenty bones inside her hand reached up,
touched the soft fabric of his devotion,
and this in turn melted her hard icy heart.
You have the most beautiful fingerprints,
he told her that day, in the mad surging crowd
eager to find last-minute Christmas gifts.
The streetlamps came on as if to emphasize,
to punctuate, yet my father's driving remains
distracted, unfocused, chaotic, irreparably bad.
The way she pronounced those vowels
threw shadows onto the back seat, where
I watched past tense mingle with present.
She was still learning, and English is no sleigh ride.
This was not some medieval triptych, men crossing rivers
and pleading their cases to woo the Chinese princess.
It was one ideogram after another, or so I liked to pretend,
filling his stoic silences with images of imagined romance.
In my mind, he drove up mountains, into valleys,
traversed steep canyons in impossible ways, nonplussed.
His lack of detail made it easier to create my own hero
out of broad brushstrokes, the lack of real knowledge.
He was the landscape changing with seasons

into something vaguely unrecognizable. He became
the names of small countries halfway across the globe,
ones I could not pronounce, ones exotic enough
for a *National Geographic* spread. Ana Song took my hand
and dipped the brush in ink. Together we made sloped lines,
dots that comprised an intimate code only she
and a billion others could figure. She said it meant "little artist."
Recalling her controlling guidance made me giddy
with excitement, and I could ignore his imminent absence
and my mother's concern about my stress eating
since he disappeared with that foreign minister lady,
the dark freckled one with a preference for satin and silk.
He is in the wilderness, my mother said, dead to me
forevermore. She made long distance calls to
relatives I would never meet, cousins of other cousins
thrice removed, people who thrived on her scandalous
reports, or merely her bragging about my latest art project,
entitled "Battle of the Shapeshifters." It won an award.
It was a woodcut of that red dress and the small flowers.
There are few details I still remember from before.
Year after year, I look at the desk where he helped me
carve my name. I let my fingers read for hidden messages,
clues as to his current whereabouts, but all I get
is the name he gave me long ago, and the way he would
squint his eyes to brace against blinding sunset
through the large windshield, accelerating beyond reason,
eager to get to the next destination.

Habits of Love and Consequence

Tendrils of contained desire
lash out like rooted weeds
in fields of passion flowers
and sprawling viburnum
as she guides me to her pleasure
with roadmaps of intention
and accelerated breath
that transport and transform me.

Changed, I am radiant effulgence
lost in throes of sense memory,
noting the pellucid redemption
this odd synesthesia provides.
This dance is growth and ritual,
a detailed liberty accumulated
through sweet surrender
masquerading as autonomy.

You've reached your destination.

Consecration

Lost in moon's shadow, we amble on,
seeking perfect ignorance,
a state of earned astonishment,
a million lost items of memory.

Every day a new beginning,
an immense reservoir of patience tried,
gathering evidence and blandishments,
striving toward change.

The loss is cumulative.

Leave vengeance to the gods
and choose your play token.
Each hour leans forward slightly,
hunched toward greater becoming.

Voyage proclaimed as salvation cruise
battles invidious plague
of rippling boredom.
Yawning. Gaping.

Each night darkness tries
to erase ruinous harm,
to provide familiar soundtrack
to wilder dreams that traduce us
into confusion, heightened collusion

between us and conscience departing
in radiance of new morning.
The wings beat loudly in retreat,
peepers bleating songs that
enchant setting moon.

This is it, the one story,
splendor of indifferent nature

infusing reality with truth,
ignored but insistent,
in the key of night air,
singing to us with radiance
of ever enlightened grace.

Baggage Claim

It was the time of revelation,
the revolution of sad confession,
telling tales of relationships gone awry,
the catalogue of human errors
and admitted imperfections
that proceeded this new "us."
He was tired of such moments,
and debated about possibly
creating wild unlikely fictions
far more interesting
than real life had provided.
He wondered if she too
felt the same exhaustion.
This is the age of no secrets,
where every story gets told
in great detail, over and over
toward some shiny oblivion.
He didn't want to know too much,
preferring the way imagination
could fill in those sensual gaps.
Let touch and scent and ignorance
converge to rule the night.
These words were no matter,
yet he felt obliged to feign interest
as she explained about that jerk
who left her for her best friend
(at least he thinks that's what she said).
He nods politely, and assumes
facial expressions appropriate
to the reception of such information.
This is crucial, meaningful sharing,
yet he wants to be somewhere,
anywhere else, loathing the
call and response of this old song,
the way he must follow-through
with some tale of equal or better

misadventures of the heart.
He longs for secrets, for solitude
without explanation, an acceptance
of existence without revisiting history.

Albert's Lament

Give me the myth of our ritual,
living in this impermanent world
with nuclear whispers on the wind.
We could be so avant-garde,
yet I don't trust the shackles
of your crazy logic and
your language riddles me with doubts.
It's a warehouse of meaningless sentiment,
a host of stereotypical responses.
When you preach to me,
I see the aged ghosts
laughing behind you.
They wait impatiently for conflict,
but here's a shock to the system:
nothing drives the plot.
Our mundane daily routine
remains uninfected by the mystical.
The miracle of precise communication
is no closer than it was before
that horribly meaningless war
and now you wave a tired arm and sigh.
Each time I discard these crutches
they appear anew, a tool to raise me
from this usual ditch, where poor-fitting
boots elevate me to this weathered rostrum
where I can continue to pretend
against all odds
to be a poet.

Recipe for Disaster

Other people who seem to have it all
discussing others who mystifyingly
took the plunge, descending fast,
riding headline to headline,
rollercoaster off the rails
prompting unsavory discussion
of how such sad feats are managed,
strength of scarf or necktie,
desperation of doorknob's
primitive methodology.
When one closes,
another opens,
then silence.

None of this pettiness is pretty.

Still the public clamors for details,
hoping to understand,
playing amateur detective,
seeking to piece together solutions.

It invokes Edwin Arlington Robinson's
call to recognize how the disease
spares no one. In the end,
status and wealth offer no immunity
from the terrible skewers
of skewed thinking
that impale contentment
in its violent wake.

You will never fully understand.

And so you get the aftermath
of shared misery and memory,
of hate and jealousy and contempt,
of praise and anecdotal evidence.

Life is a contradiction, it tells you
in extended apology, so as not to negate
all that has gone before.

Soon shock turns sullen and
more somber yet,
as legacy belies facts,
fermenting like smashed grapes
in giant cask, sweet turning sour
through measurable chemical process.

But not all formulae turn out as planned.
Real life is not your control group
and you grasp to comprehend found results.

This cannot be.

This break with the universe hurts.

Every smile seems feigned,
every mirror lies.

And as you return
to workaday rigors,
fed numbing platitudes
of feeble assurance,
you fill slowly with
sad acceptance,
wondering whose unexpected silence
inexplicably comes next.

Bildungsromantic

Let's call it privilege, this even tan
that accents your thin-lipped beauty.
You are accustomed to attention.
You have the moves down to a science.
Your curves fit the spoon of his body
like the sweet satisfaction of a puzzle piece
dropping into place. Another small victory.
Aesthetic symmetry, warmth of touch
that ignites a landslide of vertical excitement.
You close your eyes and fold in half,
all sense memory and intention,
as eager for exploration as Vasco da Gama,
that first count who first counted
curious balance of delectable favors,
spices as exotic as sin, following the wind
to foreign shore's salvation, a destination.
Carefully placed parts run your ship's master inventory
and you are safely billeted within him,
customized and sleek, a calling card for sexy
who can bend a will with well-placed laugh,
a complicated charmer from voyage launch
to arduous journey, the passage of time contracting
like heat lamps of lovers placing
soft lips on skin in expectation.
This is home, mortise and tenon
sliding into perfect joint, wave after wave
pitching with the fickle tides, yet two as one
stay locked in the beauty of collegiality
gone private. On a handshake, you agree
to conditions and then initial the codicils
that define the way this will work,
covering the face of the globe,
mouth to motor to mission statement,
Evinrude outboard propelling forward
and you smile at the feeling, the rush
of chop you leave in your wake.

Privilege unleashed, powers granted,
waves of wonder defining sea change
that can never be undone.
The child you once were
vanishes into past oblivion.
You've won.

Medusa

A walking poster for tales of misery,
she lives variants of holy horrible.

Stories of children, relatives, spouses, strangers,
all blessed with the curse of her acquaintance.

Sad tales of fates gone strangely awry,
shaking off hope with a nonchalant shrug.

I was drawn to that casual despair's beauty,
the forlorn siren song in minor key,

how strangers might find her strangely
alluring, messenger of best intentions

misshapen through anxious energies
somehow beyond her sweet control.

As she starts the next related calamity,
I am off imagining her passions in bed,

the wild call of her feral ferocity,
unleashed like hog speeding full throttle.

I smile and nod in sympathy, half listening
to story of fire, crash, untoward accident.

It's like an illness I can't quite shake,
this flailing appeal of her gloomy miasma

because after a time, her terrible tales
make daily strife seem somehow reasonable.

Big Reveal

He wakes to find
revelations in jeans pocket,
burning bushes speaking.

These are troubled times,
and more than coincident sleight of hand,
he knows he has been chosen.

The next day he is there
at his appointed place, speaking
at the farmer's market podium.

"I am not here to ruin your day,"
he explains, with a hint of apology.
The message is tacit, an elusive grail.

"It will take more than local produce
and delicious baked goods
to effect necessary change."

A vengeful God has seen enough.
When a well-dressed couple walks by,
they suddenly ignite to flame.

That sparks suburban panic,
but he stands there undaunted,
keeping calm, carrying on.

The judgment day
needs no ambient traffic,
only a message of love and tolerance.

He repeats the message,
feeding all who happen by
on homemade loaves and fresh caught fish.

"I'll return as needed,"
he tells shoppers turned disciples,
rebuking them while capturing lightning,
then taking down small table and stall.

Resolution

Every new year
was much the same:
running outside
at stroke of midnight,
breathing in cold fresh air,
gazing at stars and sky,
hoping to catch glimpse
of shiny sleek monorail,
hover-cars flying by,
Jetson-like gadgetry
suddenly arrived.
Where was it,
this era of good feeling,
vast improvement,
precedent crawling
toward becoming?
Calendar full of
blank pages,
optimistic history
awaiting days,
weeks, months.
Every new year
holding that breath,
then exhaling disappointment.
So it ever was
until one blessed moment,
staring across the square
seeing you there,
looking skyward,
breathing in
with all hope at stake:
my other,
my true heart.
As ball drops
into new year again,
we soon realize

progress can be
as simple as company,
waiting for good things
together.

Storming the Beaches in Organdy

She falls in the springtime
and decides not to get up again.

The pain is a new concentric circle,
a revelation Dante overlooked.

People tired of sheltering, zombies
wearing pajamas in public.

She counts her blessings
as if slices at the deli counter.

Gratitude by the pound
is worth the wait, she decides.

She checks the ticket;
she is hero number 67.

They are only up to 14,
so she spends the time

trying to recall
all the lyrics to *American Pie*

and their associated meanings —
footnotes to ancient history.

The lady in front of the line
has a mask that doesn't cover her nose.

Humanity's imperfections are
an endless parade of head-shakers.

And she tries harder than ever
to avoid any public restroom.

The invisible dangers float around her
hidden behind the dangers she sees.

There is no safety, but was there ever?
The illusion was fun while it lasted.

Like bright lights off spinning disco ball,
she was content in her distraction.

Now she dances in isolation,
and perhaps catches a sad glance

at herself in a dusty mirror,
expression fixed firmly in place

when the realization strikes:
this is what WWIII looks like.

Aquarium

I see fish trying to amuse us,
darting this way and that,
slivers of liquid iridescence,
colors stolen from unseen rainbows,
swimming in and out of view.
I see fish trying to confuse us,
going about their business
oblivious to audience,
leaving us wondering how
such a life of dreary dullness
is possible, as we obsess on
meetings missed by being here,
wading through waiting,
angst of being thrown from habit,
commuting our daily routine.
I see fish trying to defuse us,
take our minds from
daughter's red-faced fever,
her cries of senseless anguish
cutting right to the heart.
These silent lines that
race behind glass,
undelivered diagnoses
that we pray are nothing major,
taking us through chalk castle
luckily, without incident,
this one more time.

Change of Seasons

When I met the custodian of my desires,
she was younger than expected, and pushed
her empty grocery cart down the aisle with intention.
Her reading glasses were slightly askew, but
a knowing smile graced her face.
I was reminded of the warmth exuded
in waves from that lodge's immense fireplace,
the weekend sap ran fast through trees
toward an end of bourbon-laced maple syrup.
We sipped and savored, enamored with
the shiny taste of new knowledge shared,
delicious residual memories piling up
like fortified house of cards, standing tall
as brave beauty against inevitable death.
We were two in the garden, growing
under watchful guise of sage starlight,
laughter as amnesia-inducing bromide
hiding cracks in the foundation
spreading slowly, sure as sunrise
toward life's monumental fall.

Game With No Shot Clock

Life's no longer a contact sport,
distance constituent of
permanent remove.
Phones have deleted
social interaction
like a mismanaged app.
Instead we endorse
impossible agreements,
whine about all the ways
we cannot fathom signs.
A new generation
tied fast to fears,
we revel in misperception
slowing comprehension.
No worries, we say,
when speaking lies
that come to define us.
A team of confused individuals
won't pass the ball away,
yet we find ourselves down court,
driving hard against logic,
hoping desperate layups
still find a home.
We awake in cold sweat
standing at the foul line,
throwing up bricks
like triggered emotions,
afraid to admit
practice is needed
to change these odds,
to move ahead and beyond
this encroaching paralysis
of strange insensate loss.

III. INSIDE OUT

Long shot

We are drawn
to the allure
of the impossible.

She is Nordic perfection,
an ethereal vision, a sprite
taming woodland animals,
speaking the reindeer language.

Her very presence suggests
a play by Strindberg,
something serious,
representational, confounding.

Her ghost sonata voice
of distant cello
plays on brisk winds,
reciting whole passages
of Kafka, Camus, and Weil,
seeing bleak reality
fraught with contemplative angst.

Me, I'm more of a Shecky or Rodney,
a standup kind of guy
with roots on the lower East Side.
Overstuffed deli sandwiches
are the sloppy oeuvre of
my silly observations.
I am crowded subway car,
urban sprawl of loud sweaty complainers.

The noise, the speed, the chaos
allows no moss to grow underfoot;
mine is a cracked mirror universe
lacking serenity and perhaps
that is why I am so drawn

to her loner's solitude and peace,
those green eyes and soft curves,
her ability to sit and read and ponder.

She is peace; I am war.
Yet the same rain
envelops us in springtime,
and she'll urge me
to cast aside bruised psyche,
to feed the million hungry pigeons
gathered in Belvedere fountain.

Soundtrack swells
into blossomed crescendo
and I can almost taste
green tea on her honeyed lips,
the promise of words
before they arrange
into memorable stanzas.

Siren's silent call
is enticingly inviting,
yet disarming as romance
found within graveyards.

Inhaling the gift
of her forgiveness,
I call for more,
a gesture, a reckoning,
a miracle,

reminded that even
the occasional clunker
hoisted up from the corner
hearkens toward reverse parabola
and finds nothing but net.

Planet of the (r)Apes

The melancholy rubble
of all that once stood proud
and we went along with the story,
saluting and nodding
when it seemed easy to do so.

What did we know and when?

So many who buried knowledge
behind shaky patriarchy,
its false melancholic glory
an inadequate foundation.
Smiles confidently ignored
awkward power, inspiring
subordinate duck and cower,
looking akin to turning away,
looking the other way.

Aren't you enraged?

Day to day to another lost year,
seasons of blind abuses,
making poor excuses and
safely moving on.

Then came the turning,
slowly at first,
a quake barely registering,
a low rumble of complaint
that gathered strength
to surface secrets
needing to be heard,
that one day might
lead to the kind of change
to topple all.

This failure of gender
in plentiful mad assumptions
and unforgivable sexual plunder
seems a strange fiction,
a fetish-like affliction,
but sheer numbers say otherwise.

The entertainers, politicians,
professors, those in charge,
acting as if this was their due,
their sick advantage exercised
on a league of less fortunate targets
to satisfy predatory urges
and pseudo-supremacy,
an illusion of power
affording privilege,
a false birthright
making skin crawl accordingly.

Slowly, finally,
voices are being heard,
change forthcoming:
a legion of victims
finding expression after ages
of silent acrimony and regret.
So many (far too many)
and therein lies ignominy.

Apologies and feelings of shame
will never be sufficient
to even this brash misconduct.
We are a broken society
in need of new instruction
toward mutual respect
and overdue recognition.

These wrongs have
destroyed this planet
in ways only time

and right actions can heal.
That final scene of realization
on the beach, surrounded by
bikinis (and atolls forming),
epiphany of seismic proportion:
this is our Earth.

You finally did it, you maniacs.
You blew it up!

Learning to Read

When dusty boards proclaimed
stark elementary truths,
we saw letters as cryptic hieroglyphs.

Tiny chalk mark stars
in a blackboard of heavens,
we were quick to break
into devious alliances,
slow to learn to read.

Our souls were poisoned by
delinquent fifth graders
drinking pilfered strawberry wine
in the park across the way.
They were dangerous,
wanted others to know it.

We could see them
through the chain links
surrounding our playground.

While someone beat chalk erasers,
we yearned for Tanya and her
hot-pants-wearing friends,
donning pretend confidence
like worn denim jackets,
passing round the contraband,
being the new tragic.
We wanted it too.

Wickedness and cigarettes
seemed better than what
Weekly Readers offered,
dreams of what might be
versus what was.

Windy public school days:
collages of cliques and dioramas.
She stood her ground, all five feet of her,
gravelly voice churning out letters in
an incessant practice of cursive writing
that filled our restless sojourns.

We patrolled the grounds
as though we owned the place,
learning fast how attitude
defined playground hierarchy.
Our thunder could not rain
upon her imminent retirement.

She could wait us out,
scrawny pretenders to the throne,
certain of the harsh upcoming
headed our way.

When the cops came and arrested
those vagrant fifth graders,
we pretended halos and wings
could elevate innocence
into convincing penance.
But catechism never taught questions
like those our parents were asking.

She used the long pole to open
longer windows from the top down,
where only cooing pigeons flew by,
making sure we read our primers.

No one spoke of the blackness in our hearts,
how our heroes were angry evil poseurs
headed for places where power
evaporated like wind.

Hearing their stories third-hand,
we created legends around those

whose names ended in open vowels,
tough guys whose fathers drove big trucks.

Ignorance was our proud
common denominator
along with twenty-six letters,
the keys to expression
for unlocking a world designed
to be opened by the young.

She smiled knowingly, assured
she had wrangled another herd
of unruly steers toward the lofty plains
of second grade, and so close
to the verdant pasture herself,
far from Dick & Jane & Spot,
and the relentless chatter
of bratty first graders.
Soon she would be free
to enjoy a relaxing symphony
of sustained child-free silence.

Thinking she was happy for us,
we thanked her in ways
that were sadly inadequate,
as loud music on tiny radios
assured us that even cross-fire hurricanes
and driving rains
would somehow be all right,
that someone wanted to hold our hand.
We believed it all, now able to read the lyrics.
For a time, it made us happy inside.

Downhill Racing

The broken wheel of happiness rolls on,
skewered, lopsided body in motion
sent reeling, spinning off course.

Emcee introduces
souls ready for remedy
signed on to speak in turn,

reading aloud scribbled doodles
declaring dockets of gaping wounds
from remembered crises, world

sadly beset with chaos, gone awry
in an array of scrambled emotion:
taking notes, taking prisoners.

Yet how ever else could it be?
The gradual engagement of entropy
gains traction over time, years

folding in like creases
of a large blanket to warm
this squall of uncertain feelings,

to cover and protect against
elected horn-rimmed pretender's
latest sleight of hand.

The motion is approved,
sure as age begets wisdom.
Smattering of applause follows

as waiting begins anew
for next outsized catastrophe
to inspire incredulity
worth seeking to understand.

Requiem: Before you

I never dated a funeral director,
never made love in a body bag.
It sounds strange. It was.
Something not easily related to others,
every night another foggy secret.
When you asked me to lie corpse-like still,
when the quiet seemed almost barren,
those were times it seemed far too much.
The antiseptic feel of your examining table,
the cold couch in one of the upstairs rooms,
the long stretch in the back of the hearse.
We explored each other in loci of odd locales.
Death is a reminder to love now, you said.
And we did so often. You telling tales
of body parts discarded, the required skill
of expert cosmetician, blending
memory and reality into best
workable possibility. That also described
our times together, a relationship of
touch and lonely longing, of desperation
fueled by need. I became a phoenix,
rising from embers of a burnt-out past
to claim your naked kisses, declaring
freedom in the moment as never before.
Your regular reminders cautioned how
nothing is guaranteed, how time is rented
from the universe in hours, days, weeks,
how gratitude is a gift best expressed
without clothing. The plastic flowers
swayed in stale air, trying to escape
the old vase, the vale of tears, the grief
everlasting. Then one day it was as if
the preservative poison coursed through
your veins. It was gone, buried along
with last week's grandmother of twenty,
a peculiar memory that seems stranger yet.

Prayers and wishes could not change this
wisdom shared with countless mourners:
Eventually we all move on.

The Favorite Fish is the Dead Fish

It's a language unto itself,
expressed in green crayon
to flaunt the idea of genius
doing whatever it wants.

Possibilities are fluid,
like a serious man's puppet show,
or perhaps that's just his way
of surrendering to this world's
unreasonable controversy.

No asylum exists,
so he hides in plain sight:
on air, on line, on the big screen,
and lets puppets do all
the heavy lifting.

Real in its scary simplicity,
the message is pleasant enough
until you consider the backstory
of the spoiled boy's latent backlash
at an unforgiving populace.
Then it's just another
ordinary cry for help.

This staid patron saint of
love as boredom, wants to
live next door, convince you
of your unique importance,
offer you trophies for participation,
for breathing, for life itself.

The angry world
rejects the meek messages
of strange complacence,
of even-tempered intrusion.

Animals understand,
yet the important fish
still lies on the bottom
of the busy tank,
dead to the possibility,
transformed into
this week's lesson.
A shallow grave for
the formerly sentimental,
something we can talk out
over time, bury until talk fails us,
until failing is called success.

When entropy
takes over as beautiful day
and neighborhood is revealed
as alternate universe,
it's a temperate surprise,
an unheralded stand-in
unexpected zombie apocalypse.

The call of the mild
invades our very souls
until we float on,
belly up and staring out
into watery void:
silenced forever,
dumbfounded.

The Human Filigree

It was something of a nervous disorder,
her body generating frissons of energy
that powered, then overpowered.
Sizzling movements of angst and agita
that met in frantic dance of
restless forbearance. Yet there was
a magnetic appeal to her crazy sideshow,
an attention-gathering spotlight
that burned hot upon her, hard to ignore.
She knew this too, and savored it.
Her eclectic mannerisms were
part and parcel of her *je ne sais quoi*,
the feverish desire to fight and conquer,
a need to win that extended beyond reason.
Whatever it took, she undertook:
assumed identity, generous gift bestowed,
occasional show of steady tears. These were
weapons in her arsenal, alongside
frail beauty that demanded attention.
She now cried less, having developed
delicate acceptance of these quirks
into eclectic new equilibrium.
This strangeness is who I am, it said.
Softness contained inside hardened angles,
and hidden somewhere deeper within: a heart.

Dancing for Lions

That winter he was startled to see
the windshield wiper fluid was pink.
That year was supposed to be colder
than what the blue stuff could handle.
Climate change meant a change of color,
but change is never easily achieved.
Only the certifiable accept wholesale shifts
and take it in playful stride, like the
crazy lady who danced for the zoo lion
after jumping into his moated habitat.
King of the jungle knew not to expend effort,
wackadoodles being worthless kills, and
the incredulity of his bored expression
matched all those who watched her video.
Fact is that sometimes dumb gets lucky.
This is followed by all the other horrible news:
fires and drivebys and a roster of victims,
innocent, now dead, with family and friends
harangued by reporters' stupid questions.
Then the commercial claims some miracle drug
to improve memory has an ingredient
mined from jellyfish. Every time he sees it,
he wonders: what could those jellyfish
possibly have to remember? They wouldn't
have to deal with setting a game time lineup.
Eight different quarterbacks going down
in one fantasy roster seems like a curse,
but he points himself to the waiver wire
where holes get filled regardless.
Life is unpredictable, but still has its
happy times, pink washer fluid or not.
He turns up thermostat as game begins,
and hopes for a favorable outcome.

Holiday Apothegms

Fate follows into eternity.

Once upon mother and father ill-suited,
next thing an awkward family's dysfunction
follows. It's hardly unique.

Laying blame is a lesson in futility.

Many know such strife;
imperfection as way of life.
Yet often they will question why
normalcy has passed them by.

Thou shalt not covet thy neighbor's family.

Always the inevitable comparison
with families who seem happier,
better adjusted, well-suited to
life's sundry challenges.

Thou shalt honor thy other and thy rather.

This leads to confusion first,
then anger at perceived disrespect
or choices made and motives questioned.
It is a Gordian knot.

Try to make do in spite of graven imaginings.

We do our best with what's given.
Some walk upright and erect,
others slouch toward Bethlehem,
trying to live up to imagined potential.

Forgiveness is better than hostility.

While cure remains beyond us,
and even understanding underlying cause
seems unlikely, adjusted expectations
might help treat symptoms.

Making an effort is a possibility.

Steinweg's Erosion

In his fear of being alone,
he carried home a pretty stone,
dressed it up and called it friend
and promised days would never end.
But clocks would chime to tell his lie,
that everyone must someday die,
he waits to pawn his memory
for what might seem eternity,
a mind with rust that creaks with age
through darkened halls of chosen cage,
cane a-thumping, limp pronounced,
belief and faith soon gone, renounced.
A world of stone all turned to dust,
with friends that held the weight of trust.
So long to all he once possessed;
the rock that rolled now comes to rest.

The Work Desk Sacrament

There's far too much to do,
and unrealistic expectations
breed a weekly contempt.
This is the ritual, the chiding,
the self-knowledge that proves
awareness doesn't always act.
In fact, the browbeating lessens
over time, if only because
life demands attention, and
not according to best intents.
Breathe deep and manage
to smile at that stack ignored.
Resolve yourself to accept
your inability to achieve it all.
We are not machines, not yet,
and thus experience affords
the illusion of freedom
from plans and agendas,
a temporary respite,
apology as alibi, reassuring
that the work unfinished
will somehow someday
still manage to get done.

Elegy for Lost Alliance

There's a precarious imprecision
in memories that comprise
our relations, wavering viewpoints
that blur distinctions into emotion.
Like two songs played at once,
battling brain for attention,
ears searching for familiar
within discordant.
Your generous succor
offered up at time of
stranded desperation
was like the surprise
of oasis in mid-desert,
a rich patch of sweet succulence
that could not be real.
So I resisted, even
if this might be destiny,
you the destination, me
some visiting nomad
swaddled in bloated ego
that confounded all.
I think about that winter night
in my car, about that other time
in shadows of the basement,
the simple charms of your
unlikely stories, the purity
of your passion, the eager
willingness of your good heart.
It was magic and I turned away,
exposing the underlying aspects,
examining every facet and feature
because I am not a fan of happy,
it's not where I live.
So I made sure it would not work,
would not last, perhaps never
even occurred at all.

I look out windows
and recount what may
or may not have happened.
Young love is a matter
of indecision, of inexperience,
of holding tight against
evil inevitable,
time's bitter destruction
of once beautiful things.
You were. I was. We were.
Once and perhaps never again.
That is the tragic measure,
faults I claim long after the fact,
incessantly questioning
an inability to accept pleasure.
I cannot quiet the thoughts,
wading in sad regrets
long after I burned the bridges
that connect.
This stream of silent tears
does little to undo damage,
to cover the wide crevasse
of our undoing.
You were reluctant to give up,
to fight destiny, but I battled
until finally you fled
to never. I stand alone,
beyond forgiveness, stuck
in thickets of repeated apology
to an audience of sparrows.
You were the gift of a
beneficial universe,
and I returned the present
(now long discontinued)
shiny and new,
in youthful folly,
still unwrapped.

Morning Confession

Share your nightmares, the chemical impulses
that rule your slumbering body, the psychological
underpinnings of how your brain embraces the day.
I will listen eagerly, wanting to know you better,
to understand the fragile fears that build your
tentative house of cards that cowers inside
closetful of stylish and matching outfits,
the decoupage of personality you've glued
together thus far, colorful and sexy and wild.
Talk to me of the thunder that crashes your
expectations, the lightning that illuminates
storms at the edge of solace, the story
of when the rock star stole your innocence
inside the luxury hotel. These are the constellations
we try to piece together, the ancient meanings
borrowed, blue, and wedded to the weather
of our ways, the peaceful circle thrumming
with desire that only our nether halves admit,
bark and bluster reduced to somatic quiescence.

Excellence is Our Motto

In these hyperbolic times,
there is comfort in hearing
that you are the very best.
Forget that such claims
are wildly unfounded,
and that mediocrity
has been elevated to art form.
Inflate the numbers,
for everything is extra credit.
Here's a trophy for growth,
another for progress,
a third for the kind of grades
sure to get you into a good college.
Empathy and compassion
can be learned if required.
Creativity and service
can be spun like a crazy yarn,
and we'll all outdo each other
in the most charitable of ways.
Pad that resume big-time,
do not differentiate
concerning extra-curriculars:
play sports, join clubs,
be a band or theater geek,
or at least show up for
one of the meetings.
It's not so much what you do,
as appearance of good intentions.
Excellence is trending,
and a whole class of heroes
of compromised quality
is ready to take that
next step forward,
leaping with practiced confidence
into the steep abyss
of harsh reality.

The Nature of Inquiry

We are all butterflies flitting aimlessly
from flower to flower in lavender fields,
harboring secrets even from ourselves.
What instinct drives us to fly?
What is this why we cannot let go?
Searching shadow's flicker
on walls of candlelit rooms.
Not a clue to be found.
Who is the love that rocks
our landscape with gale force winds?
Where are we headed, what are
we wishing for underneath
shadows of passing stars?
Who will guide our lost hearts?
Every day a new river flows across
anachronistic fish who seem to know better.
What are they swimming toward?
An army of the unique, marching
toward individual oblivion.
This is the cloud of dust that defines us,
the familiar melody stuck in our head,
the song that plays on and on,
relentless and redeeming,
yet we own it through
humming the refrain
as if it held answers.

Senescence

It's never what you expect.
The event that changed the world
happened against backdrop
of beautiful Tuesday morning.

It's never the same again.
Each moment brings change:
the dark shroud grows blacker,
the introspection deeper,
the prayers more desperate.

It's never an invitation to silence.
We're expected to speak our minds,
voice thoughtful concerns, formed
in calm reasonable tones, outside
plagues of fearful panic that
infect the ubiquitous daily media.

It's never going to go as planned.
The breathless realizations as
things go awry, deteriorate
into surprising downward spiral
as rapid descent occurs.

It's never what you expect.
So savor the safe illusions, make
each grateful moment count
as silent countdown shouts
background noise, ticking,
ticking, ticking away.

IV. INSIDE OUTRAGE

Peripeteia

Because of global warming, you get
weather by the minute, phones shrieking

flash flood warnings like AMBER alerts,
spreading panic and fear like hard rain.

You kneel as if under a tree, awaiting
that fatal lightning strike, a power surge

to freeze time forever, a moment of
glass-shattering clarity, surfacing after

holding each breath to show control
over a world of chaotic mass confusion.

The rumbles and darkened sky are
preludes to false relief, a faulty belief

that a solution exists. You cry at times,
afflicted with the sadness that prevails

in news stories that attack and affect us all.
That crumbling country, celebrity monster,

the nascent whisper, the gut decision,
the absolute stupidity of beginning again.

This empty life seems filled with revenge,
blame, and the steeped ashes of past envy.

You line up for salvation, redemption
doled out by forgiving gods on a tight

holiday schedule. You hear the sounds,
see bats flying like crazy trapeze

impresarios, and you reluctantly
realize that every aspect of your life

is based on a true story. You sense it,
let it wash over you, a darkness

familiar and comforting, a hope for change
that might yet pardon this fast falling spiral.

The Unearthing

You emerge from the garden
renewed, refreshed,
smelling of soap and
floral essence,
as package proclaims.

You came from the city,
urbane and affected,
a child of another era
lacking proper causes
to serve in heartfelt protest.

So you took the easy path:
less-traveled, who can say?
Your brother calls it
surrender to suburbia.
You wear a convincing smile
with that sundress.

In this place of grazing deer
and lurking ticks, you learn
names of plants and trees,
the fauna who trespass
their usurped environs,
singing to the moon of
older, better times
nightly, without hesitation.

Their history is not yours to share.

Your story is to subvert and deny,
bury your real self beneath
these mounds of rich, fertile soil,
in planters that show a colorful array
of sun-drenched seasonal excuses.

It looks welcoming. It invites
compliments, comments on
verdant digits, a quiet appreciation
of nature as savior, sprouting
beauty at every turn.

But you know it's a lie.

This resplendence of pink, yellow, and white
is asking red questions. You water them
to silence uncertainties, quell
inner lightning and fire reflected
in these variegated fronds.

As each variety blooms in turn,
you turn away, goddess weeping
for spells not cast, mortal mistakes,
penance observed and plucked when ripe
in harvest of realization.

You become a stranger to yourself,
weathered by time and compromise.
The mirror offers no solace,
only your eyes show evidence
of seeds, spark from an age
before you threw in the trowel.

Heart wars with mind now.
You search for ripe magnificence
of caring, of compassion,
when fawn teeters on untried limbs,
stumbling toward grace.

It was you once, kneeling in the grass,
enraged by ideas, dreaming of
revolution and restitution,
kernels of truth germinating
in green blades
bending to wind.

You turn the soil slowly,
stirring up the landscape,
ignoring the immensity
of wasted potential,
seeds never planted,
for there's always a season ahead,
chances to realize youthful promises
beyond restoring lawn and order.

Practicum

Once gravedigger
puts on the forceps,
clocks start ticking,
sand sifts down
the big hourglass.
The race is on.
Not a soul wants
to face harsh truths.
Instead we explore
a world of distraction:
sports, knowledge, rules,
regulations, theories, recipes.
We analyze, we proselytize.
We judge and are judged,
yet we cry out
for companionship.
Misery loves company
and hates isolation.
Let us face that fear
of the unknown together,
or better yet collapse
in a spent heap after
raucous bout of
unbridled passion.
Love is every answer.
Let us dream and be dreamt of,
close contact as best defense.
Fight loneliness
and conquer death
momentarily
via la petite mort,
a training exercise
that's proven effective;
a touch of pleasure
delays inevitable reckoning
already fast on its way.

Three Feet and a Yard

Two shadows were arm-wrestling in the corner.
I entered the room under the pretense of trying
to find what was lost. I grew up in this place,
when it had ugly shag carpeting and a certain
texture to the wallpaper. My mother was
the adversary of fashion then, and she purchased
a closet full of leisure suits to have me sustain
the legacy. Spirits spat at the choices made,
the colors, the patterns, the absolute wrongness
of the combinations. Others in the same situation
would have invented *Garanimals* or the like,
but all I could do was wear the gray polyester
and try to remain far from any open flames.
Life was a myopic journey of sad reproach,
and I fell in love with the white trash tragedy
of our starter home. The local billboard
became my ancient Egyptian obelisk,
but instead of answers, all I got was
the toll-free number of a mystical chiropodist,
which I promptly memorized like a mantra.

Talking

Let's do things,
not talk about them, she says.
Then she talks endlessly.

Nothing is as bad as love.
Always in love,
suffering from love.
Always suffering.

She is full of empty promises
that keep us apart.
Maybe she needs a
woman who can better relate.

I am close enough in age
to understand horrors of young love.

So why are we sitting in this
sad restaurant at one in the morning
in a city that magnifies the problem?

Confrontation works.
See if there is love in her eyes.
It can't be hidden.

Love is a god, she says,
making everything work.
An effective but angry god.

I feel ancient, she says.
Yet she doesn't look bad.
Finding another would be a good idea,
but she can't.

She is in such a state.
Talking to stay alive.

If this is being done now,
she will do it again.
Be ready.

Confront her or don't love her.
Hiding is insane.
It's not love in her eyes,
it's something else.
Something with great meaning
that I don't understand.

Vacant consolations expressed:
don't worry; you'll get her back.
It's never too late.
Never.

Perpetuity

In muddy remains of what once was a river,
two boys search for relics of another time.
They find a headless doll and a water-damaged
issue of some amateur porn magazine.

The pictures are hard to discern.
A suburban housewife is naked
except for high heels and a watch.
She seems late for something.

There is a letters column that the boys
read aloud to one another.
One reader named *Frisky* laments
the inevitability of nuclear Armageddon.

His logic extends to the idea that,
when one world ends, anything
and everything is possible, encouraged,
including indulging strange fetishes.

Another man called *Frequent Flier*
talks of hand jobs from flight attendants
and of joining the mile high club,
even with his wife back in her aisle seat.

The boys toss back their findings.
That past is useless for their present.
They trudge upstream, find the
body of what was an acoustic guitar.

One remarks that it's probably Jason's,
known for his quick abandonment
of hobbies that require effort or study.
He has no patience for anything.

They are not known for it either,
but pills help them focus in school,
and extra time assures a level playing field
in this march toward collegiate endgame.

They step tentatively, battling the mud
and how it seems to suck them down into
the moist brown nothingness that
once held fish eggs and more.

They are oblivious to their surroundings,
eager for new ways to be entertained.
This is dumb, one says aloud, and the other
grunts his stolid agreement.

They decide to return home
where video games might kill an hour,
stave off the stack of homework
some optimistic teachers assigned them.

Let them savor the sweet boredom of youth,
the very concept of leisure that will desert them
when reality rears its sharpened claws
and time leaves inevitable scars upon them.

This is the unidentifiable pain of innocence,
the universal language of languor and laziness
that marks a new generation in different ways
that reminds us all of ways of our own.

Blocked

According to Block Universe Theory,
our perception of time is wrong —
it blinds us to its true nature:
a four-dimensional block.

If all time is simultaneous,
past, future, and present,
all going on always
relative to me and my experience,

then let me travel back
to correct mistakes;
let me travel ahead
to learn valuable lessons,

let me share this moment
with you forever,
not letting pretender Time
come along to destroy it.

For time is not on our side,
nor is it of the essence.
It won't tell, it won't march on,
nor will it heal all wounds.

Let us celebrate the infinity
of our limited mortality,
the strands of plural occurrence
that appear as false chronology.

It's only a man-made construct
to help our feeble brains
to better understand
the inestimable unknowable:

in that, it's much like a poem.

Legerdemain

Remembered day in city unknown:
morning knocking like vindictive swindler,
telling tales of absent landlords,
neighborhood's dares and temptations
reduced to piles of broken glass.
It was a heritage of trickery,
a pride of foreign con artists
galloping back alleyways
toward hopeful redemption.
Across the way was the club
Urban Deliria, offering shelter
to hoodlums with Rickenbackers
masquerading as punks. We hear
breathy contortions of complaint,
remnant results of last night's
bring your own bass gathering,
anger trailing daylight like
pretentious cloud of steamed milk,
the promise of cappuccino
ordered but never served.
In sullen memories
of black leather midnight,
we were a minority of true
surrounded by hatred,
dancing to escape slick reality.
Pervasive piercings
shone in klieg lights
as snares pounded tattoos
that had us longingly dreaming
of some illusory home,
a world of fried dough
and confectioner's sugar
summoned for healing
after stale dark hours
of deeply imagined hurt.

The Classroom

We ask them to identify global issues
at a time when their own lives *are* the global issue,
when identity comes masked and at a remove
measured and circumscribed for safety
according to the latest recommendations.

This remains a social place, as it must,
where exchanged ideas ignite the fires
that fuel internal growth alongside
the social and the physical, and we bear witness
daily to the awesome and real act of becoming.

Now we are in a prolonged fugue, a limbo
wherein they better grasp the repetitive hopes
of Vladimir and Estragon, awaiting further instruction.
As news brings forth each sobering tidal wave
of rising numbers, it grows harder to pretend.

Every week brings a new normal.
Haggard-looking administrators roam hallways
with official clipboards of doom,
asking four questions to trace
the trails of those not virally passed over.

And all the while we take attendance,
having learned to smile with our eyes,
and dispense daily lessons that pale
against these larger life lessons
that challenge and instruct us all.

Here in our smart modern classrooms
we muster the safest havens we can manage,
sharing screens and hearts and minds,
knowing that with each period's gathering
comes a strong dose of social healing.

All pandemics come to an end,
the wisdom of the ages suggests.
Yet until that ancient saw becomes reality,
there's a remedy called the classroom
that brings the dream closer, uniting us in wisdom.

With this new world comes higher order questions
 that Bloom's taxonomy never considered.
Through shared crisis comes unmasked truths:
together we feel shared love that helps us through
what often seems these most trying of times.

Meeting Joan of Arc For Brunch

*The enormity of eternity
is treacherous,* she confides.
You cannot trust a soul.
I disagree and tell her so.
We touch hands, a gesture
of respect and affection,
because we come from
such different places.
My stillness melts glaciers,
her phosphorescence
lights the way for many.
Hers is a delicate frenetic,
a graceful kinesthesia,
heartbeat breathing in/out
through long summer of motion.
It has been a dynamic progression,
a true peripeteia:
earning the numbers,
learning the formulae,
privy to the inside joke.
She laughs and it is complete,
this cycle of discovery.
Yet the chorus cannot act
upon the players and the
hidden lawyers are putting out
forest fires started elsewhere.
Dreams are jury-rigged accordingly,
and the primrose path of
whitewashed future
gets sold at an auction's discount.
Trust in yourself, I tell her.
Remedy concerns. Trust the code.
Seek forgiveness. Know contrition.
Even as I speak, I know it cannot be.
History repeats for a reason.

Discretion and valor notwithstanding,
she is now off to battle and
my good wishes will mean nothing
on the beachhead of the practical.
I unlock the cage and set her free,
even though she is the one with the key.

Expedition

Morning light casts shadows
on shallows before me
as I cast off, breathe in the coolness
and head out beyond coastal banks
into depths of greater confusion.
Miles of brackish green drink sun
as if seized with unquenchable thirst,
so I turn the rudder toward the
journeying orb as if it might
offer a glimpse into where
strange sideways halibut
hide out in unison.

My ancestors would ride
this same type of small craft
into tempestuous ocean,
courting wild waves into
rough pas de deux, but still
bending and breaking,
returning triumphant
with prize catch in tow,
food enough to keep locals
sated for a week or more.

Now there's community no more,
ragged shoreline sold off
to builders of condos on time share,
mako sharks of marketing
hawking deals on promises,
handshakes, and artist renditions.

Gulls and small birds point the way
toward some surface activity,
but often that's a false positive,
sign of feeding humpbacks below,

air bubbles gushing with hope.
More likely than not,
I'll return empty-handed.

A taller man could rest on the moon,
she said, look down and see schools
of fish in session. So wise,
as if she hadn't already invested
in that electronic finder
measuring best locations
with solar-powered
high intensity GPS.
It doesn't help any.

Those paying close attention
can see through the native wisdom,
folklore passed off as sage phrases
like bad horoscopes and sailor rhymes.

At least my skin turns brown and
the sun warms inner organs.
It is a good day to fish, I say,
paraphrasing Papa but meaning
every saline syllable, smiling
as if I somehow knew better,
pretending become an easy act,
gunning the motor
and stretching out toward
a greater infinity.

Have You Graded The Essays Yet?

My student says what the main character does is of the
upmost importance. It's not so much just nature versus nurture,
but also the fact that he has experienced great neglect
in his formative years. It's a schema, she tells me, one
that she learned about in psychology or maybe
theory of knowledge. It's all theoretical, that much I realize,
especially in this day of age. The same way someone has
theoretically absconded with all the possessive apostrophes
and many of her commas. There, their, they're, and affect/effect
are lost causes, for all intensive purposes. A grammatically
correct paper would be the sign of a looser, which I envision
as a spineless moray of a creature, barely able to sit upright
and borrow a pen from a classmate. She plays fast and loose
with the conventions of standard English usage.
Does spelling count? She wants to know, defiantly,
as if standing up to the metaphorical shackles of the
grammar man. Unable to remember one character's name,
she spells it three different ways within the essay. And
edward estlin cummings, your sweet lower case victory
is assured, now that today's generation Z has proclaimed
the death of capital letters for things like names and
the letter i. Still, I mark on, my red pen signaling changes
to a generation seemingly immune to them. Writing
is a lost art, along with reading. The practical wisdom
inquires along the lines of, "Why read when I can
sparknote or *shmoop* it?" And while we're pursuing
the inanity of adolescent logic, let's hear another volley
of questions regarding literary choices: "Why don't we read
anything with a happy ending?" Learning life lessons is of the
upmost importance, I remind them, knowing that there is
a special place in heaven for those that have to grade
high school English essays. "Does everything have to be
included in the thesis? Do we need an introduction *and*
a conclusion? How many paragraphs would be a good number?"
I try to maintain a semblance of reasoned wisdom when

I tell them "Eleventeen," and that's why I am English, not math.

History's Assurance

The pandemic gods awaken
from their hundred-year's slumber and sigh.

While their inclination once was laughter,
they now harden according to what times demand.

They search for a silver thread of truth,
of music teased from mass cacophony,

the notes a sweet chorus of souls rising
from crowded ICUs to roomy heavens.

Hearts shaken with devastation
beat a rhythm of late acknowledgment

as migration from fear to recognition
spreads virally, traced by salt tears

that season an otherwise bland
palate of bloated overgrown time.

The pantheon delivers random storms,
rumbles of thunder presaging panic

of lost wonder, of world at risk,
society floating off from innocence.

The pandemic gods dissipate
like clouds creeping in midnight sky,

then blow across the firmament
to reform as a breath of hope

for those inhaling to survive:
a new song will arrive.

Inside Outrage

Hard to grasp what illumines others
when all still holds such awful weight.
Of late, time drags on: slow, glacial, austere,
through dregs of weary confusion.

These are what dreary remnants remain
of broken dreams shattered and incomplete,
a million shards recast and gathered up,
then bagged away as dated rubbish.

Each day's able accretion creeps
nearer a state of belabored abeyance.
Moments twitch minutes of restless sleep,
while thick fog envelops existence.

Calendar blocks out seasons extended:
days seem like weeks — protracted, emended.
Windswept craters howl tenuous dirge
of sweet facile human impermanence.

Fickle moon travels nightly apace,
travail turned to travesty in Mars' dark red place,
midnight's blue majesty overseeing orbits
of satellites' outer space pasture.

What never adds up are the measures of men:
all gesture, no pleasure grinding out sad routines.
Raging against fears that daily alarm them
in harsh world of mediocre median's mean.

The current depression is adopted devotion;
Seclusion, accepted defeat's slow erosion.
And still every day to avoid the implosion
one simply pretends to go through the motions.

Re-Cycled

It begins *in the end*,
which is confusing enough,
but logical in many awkward ways.
A life lived long enough can result
in deterioration, loss of control,
reducing eldest back to
pseudo-infancy.

In the end, you.
Who else? This makes sense.
When all is said and done,
what more does anyone have
but the essence that has been
called you. A layered identity
that defines a life in its various
and sundry iterations.
So very true; so very you.

In the end, you must.
Many dictums, so little time.
Even toward the end,
there is no let-up on
rules to be followed.
laws to be heeded,
taxes to be paid,
social customs to be minded.
Only death frees you from
the justice of must,
simply because.

In the end, you must forgive.
After all those many years
of countless sins and misdemeanors,
of poor intentions and iffy results,
of attitude problems, bad habits,

worse choices, regrets and things
done either accidentally or on purpose.
Penance, absolution, a clearing of the score
is most desirable, if even possible.
Make a list, and try to work your
systematic way through this
important and lengthy apologia.

In the end, you must forgive yourself.
This, alas, is the hardest part.
Easier to make your peace with
even the worst of enemies
because it is the end, and you must
come at long last to a loving reckoning
not easily achieved. Look in the mirror
and know you tried.
Every life is a beautiful tapestry
of failure and victory,
wins and losses, pain and pleasure.
But find your way to love the one
who bears the brunt of blame.
Yes, this is the most difficult task,
but also the most necessary.

In the end, you must forgive yourself.
In the end, you must forgive yourself.
In the end, you must forgive yourself.

Notes

"TripTik" (pg. 42) draws inspiration from the Larry Levis poem, "Childhood Ideogram."

"Talking" (pg. 98) is inspired by Kenneth Koch's poem, "Talking to Patrizia."

About the Author

Gary Glauber is a widely published poet, fiction writer, teacher, musician, former music journalist, business owner, and sportswriter. He is the author of five poetry collections: *Small Consolations* (Aldrich Press), *Worth the Candle* (Five Oaks Press), *Rocky Landscape With Vagrants* (Cyberwit Press), *A Careful Contrition* (Shanti Arts), and *Inside Outrage* (Sheila-Na-Gig Editions). He also has published two chapbooks: *Memory Marries Desire* (Finishing Line Press) and *The Covalence of Equanimity* (SurVision Books), a winner of 2019 James Tate Poetry Contest.

Glauber has had a career featuring over 500 published poems, many of which have been nominated for *Best of the Net* and *Pushcart Prizes*. He holds an MFA degree in Playwriting from Carnegie-Mellon University, and he has contributed work to a number of celebrated anthologies. He can often be seen taking part in local and online readings, sharing his work in a variety of venues, including the *New York Poetry Festival* on Governor's Island. Over the years, he also has been associated with several larger poetry projects including *Found Poetry Review*'s 'Pulitzer Remix,' wherein he created a diverse cornucopia of 30 poems in one month derived from and inspired by the assigned source material of Richard Russo's classic novel *Empire Falls*.

He loves to share his passions for literature, journalism, and music, and he is grateful for the energy and enthusiasm that his students bring to the classroom. These past few years have been unlike any other, presenting challenges from moment to moment, and proving the resourceful resilience of the human spirit. As we slowly emerge into the cautious parameters of this new normal, Glauber remains an astute observer of life's absurdities, eager to capture the ever-elusive magic of the creative muse again.

CPSIA information can be obtained
at www.ICGtesting.com
Printed in the USA
BVHW091720060522
636309BV00010B/882